OSTRICHES

by Rose Davin

Raintree is an imprint of Capstone Global Library Limited, a company incorporated in England and Wales having its registered office at 264 Banbury Road, Oxford, OX2 7DY – Registered company number: 6695582

www.raintree.co.uk
myorders@raintree.co.uk

Text © Capstone Global Library Limited 2017
The moral rights of the proprietor have been asserted.

All rights reserved. No part of this publication may be reproduced in any form or by any means (including photocopying or storing it in any medium by electronic means and whether or not transiently or incidentally to some other use of this publication) without the written permission of the copyright owner, except in accordance with the provisions of the Copyright, Designs and Patents Act 1988 or under the terms of a licence issued by the Copyright Licensing Agency, Saffron House, 6–10 Kirby Street, London EC1N 8TS (www.cla.co.uk). Applications for the copyright owner's written permission should be addressed to the publisher.

ISBN 978 1 4747 3659 6
20 19 18 17 16
10 9 8 7 6 5 4 3 2 1

British Library Cataloguing in Publication Data
A full catalogue record for this book is available from the British Library.

Editorial Credits
Marysa Storm and Alesha Sullivan, editors; Kayla Rossow, designer; Ruth Smith, media researcher; Kathy McColley, production specialist

Photo Credits
Capstone Press: 6; Dreamstime: © Anke Van Wyk, 19; Newscom: National News/ZUMAPRESS, 21; Shutterstock: Andrzej Kubik, 24, Asian Images, 2, 24, CHIEW, 15, Dominique de La Croix, 7, Elsa Hoffmann, 17, Ivanov Gleb, 5, JONATHAN PLEDGER, 13, optionm, 22, paula French, 1, Rudmer Zwerver, 10, Ryan M. Bolton, 9, SABPICS, 11, Sergei25, cover, back cover

Note to Parents and Teachers

The Meet Desert Animals set supports national curriculum standards for science related to life science and ecosystems. This book describes and illustrates ostriches. The images support early readers in understanding the text. The repetition of words and phrases helps early readers learn new words. This book also introduces early readers to subject-specific vocabulary words, which are defined in the Glossary section. Early readers may need assistance to read some words and to use the Table of Contents, Glossary, Read more, Websites, Comprehension questions and Index sections of the book.

Printed and bound in China.

MORAY COUNCIL
LIBRARIES &
INFO.SERVICES

20 41 84 64

Askews & Holts

J598.524

CONTENTS

Look out! 4
Big birds 8
Time to eat 12
Life cycle 14

Glossary 22
Read more 23
Websites 23
Comprehension questions 24
Index 24

LOOK OUT!

Here comes a giant bird.

It's not flying. It's running!

Ostriches can run 70 kilometres

(43 miles) per hour.

Wild ostriches live in deserts and grasslands in Africa. Ostriches live together in groups called flocks.

● where ostriches live

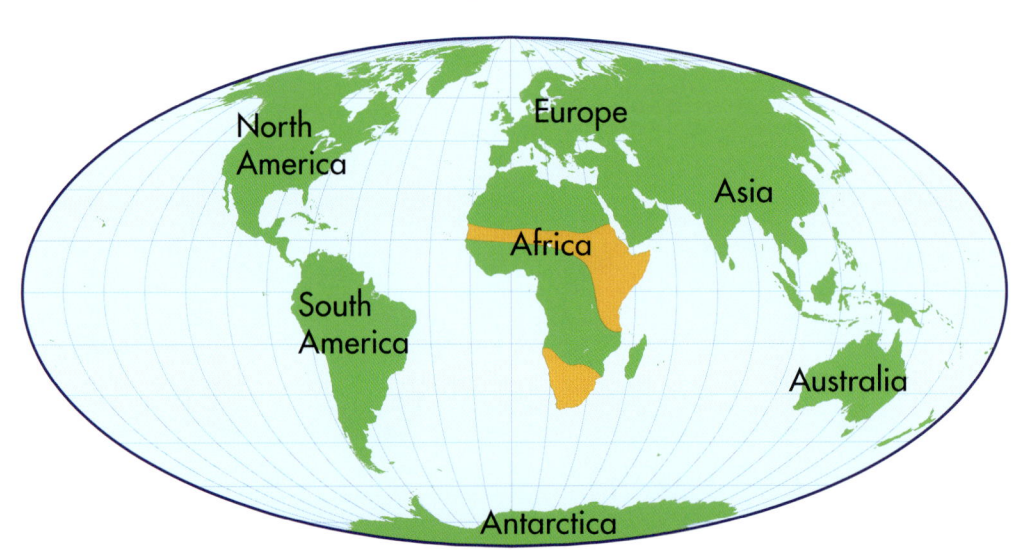

North America
Europe
Asia
Africa
South America
Australia
Antarctica

BIG BIRDS

Ostriches are the biggest birds in the world. They can be about 3 metres (9 feet) tall.

Ostriches have short wings.

But ostriches are too heavy to fly.

Male ostriches have black and white feathers.

Female ostriches have brown and grey feathers.

Ostriches have big eyes. They have long necks and skinny legs.

TIME TO EAT

Ostriches eat grass, leaves and insects.

Sometimes they catch lizards and snakes.

They also eat sand and pebbles.

This helps the birds grind their food.

LIFE CYCLE

All of the flock's hens lay eggs in one nest. Each egg weighs about 1,500 grams (3 pounds).

A female ostrich is called a hen.

She sits on the eggs during the day.

A male ostrich sits on the eggs at night.

Eggs hatch in about 45 days.

Ostrich chicks are about as big as chickens. Parents use their wings to shelter chicks from the sun. Males protect chicks from predators.

Cheetahs, leopards and hyenas hunt ostriches. But one kick from an ostrich can kill a predator. Ostriches can live more than 30 years in the wild.

Glossary

desert area of dry land with few plants; deserts receive little rain

feathers one of the light, fluffy parts that covers a bird's body; feathers protect an ostrich's skin and keep it warm during cool desert nights

grassland open land covered mostly by grass; grasslands have few trees

hen female bird

hyena large animal of Asia and Africa that looks like a dog

insect small animal with a hard outer shell, six legs, three body sections and two antennae; most insects have wings

predator animal that hunts other animals for food

shelter to protect

Read more

Fantastic Facts About Ostriches, Miles Merchant (Thought Junction Publishing, 2015)

Ostrich (Grassland Animals), Louise Spilsbury (Raintree, 2012)

Ostriches (Super Species), Grace Hansen (Abdo Kids, 2016)

Websites

http://www.bbc.co.uk/nature/life/Ostrich

Learn facts about ostriches on the BBC website.

http://animals.nationalgeographic.com/animals/birds/ostrich/

View photos and discover cool facts about ostriches.

Comprehension questions

1. Why do you think all ostrich hens put their eggs in one nest?
2. How do male ostriches help the flock?
3. How does the ability to run fast help an ostrich?

Index

Africa 6
chicks 18
deserts 6
eating 12
eggs 14, 16
eyes 10
feathers 10
flocks 6, 14

flying 4, 8
grasslands 6
height 8
hens 16
legs 10
predators 18, 20
running 4
wings 8, 18